CU00956311

MORE VOICES PLEASE (PRAAT SAAM ASSEBLIEF)

A bilingual anthology by

George Hector

For my six children and their wives/ husbands and partners, Wayne and Wendy, Jason and Stacy, Danielle and Jody, Chad and Melissa, Justine, and Kirsten and Wade, but especially for my eight fabulous grandchildren, Stephanie, Gabriella, Seth, Summer, Joel, Hugo, Josh, and Hudson.

I am forever grateful to the language teachers, both English and Afrikaans, who opened my mind to the wonder of literature, language, and poetry. These were my Primary School teachers at the Independent Congregational School and Sunnyside Primary School, my High School teachers at both Alexander Sinton High and Belgravia High. These High School teachers were Mr Strydom, Mr Lochner, Mr John Scott, and Mr Piet Philander. Mr Abu Desai and Mr Gert Oosthuizen at Hewat College of Education are legends in their lifetime. At UWC I was privileged to sit at the feet of Ikey van der Rheede, Tony Links, and Jakes Gerwel.

Thanks to the social butterfly who networked with energy abounding to get the anthology off the ground, my niece, Meghan.

And then there were the many friends and colleagues, too numerous to mention, who enthused over getting this work into print.

CONTENTS

FOREWORD

Writing poetry is not a job you report to every day, and get on with providing a service, or fulfilling production. It is vested in the mystery of inspiration, that which exists in the realm of the immeasurable, the mysterious, the gloriously unexpected. In a globe of 8 billion people, that moment of inspiration is yours, and yours alone, and that in itself, is a miracle.

It's a silly statement, a cliché, of people often saying, you're a poet, you just don't know it. The works that I have written is inspiration I draw from just observing the community, its struggles, its social reality, the tragic divide between the poor and the rich, and the concomitant suffering and pain I so often observe amongst our South African people. And as a keen gardener and naturalist, great moments of inspiration often cross my path, the birds, the flowers, the vegetable garden, the visiting endangered Leopard Toads, the bees and other insects, amongst others. Often, a moment in time is captured in one's observations, but is also sometimes lost, because it is not put down on paper. For example, one day, at the traffic lights of a shopping Mall in Cape Town called Kenilworth Centre, I saw a young man hawking with Candyfloss, and the thought of sameness came to mind, we're so alike, but we focus so much on our differences. I pulled off the road, and wrote the seed thoughts of the poem, Ghoemahare. Ghoemahare is what Candyfloss is called in Afrikaans in the vernacular. Spookasem is another delicious idiomatic equivalent in Afrikaans, spook being a ghost, and asem meaning breath! So whether it is Ghoemahare, Candyfloss, or Spookasem, it's one and the same, and yet we focus so much on our differences! It is hoped that some of my work might inspire others to explore the latent creative talent within them. But remember, seize the moment of inspiration, for it might be lost on you so quickly! Technology, much maligned sometimes, can serve great and useful purposes. I have opened a file on my smart phone, and when I receive a moment of inspiration, I access the file there and then, write the seed thoughts down, and then refresh, review, and refine. The latter actions are when the hard work really begins, but when the final product is eventually recorded, the sense of fulfilment is sublime.

I grew up as a young child on my parents' knees, in a totally Afrikaans environment. So my mother-tongue is ingrained in me. But a blessing in South Africa is its bilingualism, in our case English and Afrikaans. But in other contexts there are similar bilingual realities, for example, isiXhosa and English. Out of acknowledgement to those perhaps not so well-versed in Afrikaans, I will attempt to do a free translation of some of the poems I wrote in Afrikaans. I will also, as a footnote, socio-politically sketch the context of some of my work.

Writing poetry is 10% inspiration and 90% perspiration. One experiences an inspiring moment, the seed thought of the poem, and then the hard work starts, hours and hours of reflection, editing, more editing, until one is satisfied with the finished product.

Much of my work is unashamedly socio-political, the agony and pain I experience at the suffering of our people, and how, despite our new democratic social order, there just seems to be no end in sight at the intensifying poverty of the greater majority of our people, and it is getting worse. Apartheid was an economic doctrine aimed at enriching 5% of the population, and using statutory means, passing laws in the minority parliament, to ensure that the riches remained in the hands of those classified white. Apartheid, and its cousins, colonialism and imperialism, was never an ideology, it was no belief system, it was just a vicious economic system to ensure the continuing subjugation of our people. And now, this being the greatest irony of all, under democracy the gap between the rich and the poor is widening with the passing of every day, the rich being largely white, with a spattering of politically connected blacks and a few genial black entrepreneurs, and the poor living a life of misery and hell in townships and informal settlements. And there is no end in sight, fundamentally no improvement in the lives of the greater majority.

The Covid 19 pandemic of the third decade of the 21st century was such a huge wake-up call, amplifying how ravaging it is to be poor. No access to nutrition, no access to basic services like electricity and running water, no access to quality healthcare, and certainly no access to quality education, and how all these factors affect the quality of life. Quite a few of my works are based on my experiences, observations and perceptions of the impact of the pandemic.

And if my work is contentious and even evokes outrage in some quarters, I make no apology for it. The Good Book says that it is only the truth that can set us free, and the truth is that we can only collectively prosper if an enabling environment is created for all. Let us take the schooling system in South Africa as an example. By using the statutory determinants (in particular the South African Schools Act), two systems stand in juxtaposition in the public education sector. Those who have inherited the former Model C system under apartheid, with its rich infrastructure and human capital resources, and now sustained by school fees that, in some cases, exceed that of the universities! (and here I talk about public schools in statutory terms). And on the other hand is a failing system for the rest of the nation's children, with 80% of the Grade 4 learners unable to read with comprehension, and children drowning in faeces in pit latrines, also known as long-drop toilets. The late Graeme Bloch, in his book, The Toxic Mix, a seminal work on the failing education system in South Africa, put it so succinctly when he wrote: "Schooling in South Africa is a national disaster. ... Worse still is the tragedy that our schools are re-inforcing the social and economic marginalization of the poor and vulnerable." (Bloch, G: The Toxic Mix: 58. Tafelberg, 2009)

I hope my introductory comments aren't interpreted as vitriolic anger, but rather as an expression of hope of working together to build a better future for all. And as the events in July 2021, the terrifying looting in Kwazulu-Natal and Gauteng revealed, we are running out of time to save the beautiful dream of Archbishop Emeritus Desmond Tutu, one of the Rainbow Nation of God.

George Hector

December 2022

ENDORSEMENTS

As I try to hold back the tears, my heart is filled with nostalgia. A masterpiece in its own right! What a fitting Anthology, a must-read for all who care about our beloved country. "My gemoed skiet vol, oorstelp van vreugde." (My heart is full with the joy of reading this work.)

JEREMY FREDERICKS

A rollercoaster of emotions pushing me to wrestle anew with my understanding of humanity from creation to dust. This explosive ride, though brief, continues still! A resounding commendation to this inspirational "...Voice..."

REV LES MATHYS

George Hector's "More Voices Please" personifies and is an extension of his character, jovial dry humour, a smile, and the engaging conversations coming through in the poems he has written. I am drawn into his world, his mind, his heart, and his compassion for the poor and the marginalized. Yet the lightheartedness, in part, he expresses in the poem "Sipho and Gogo" intrigues me. I yearn to read more, learn more, experience more ......

ANDRE ALEXANDER (Author of the book "The Turning Point")

This Anthology reflects deep concern for the socio-political situation in South Africa, past and present. Through striking family, community-based, and nature images, it illuminates the painful effects of the social order. It also highlights the importance of caring family relationships, and the development of values such as diligence, justice, compassion, loyalty, kindness. love for humanity, thoughtfulness ...
I endorse this relevant and thought-provoking Anthology.

JOHN GEORGE SWART

Rich in variety, this brilliant Anthology will delight, and stir the emotions of every reader. Many poems offer deep truths to ponder. A classic contribution to poetry from the writer's heart!

ANTHEA DE VOUX

This compelling Anthology weaves a compelling tapestry of socio-political content and musings on cherished memories, thus inviting reflection on, and connection with, being a person of colour in South Africa.

DR TRUNETTE JOSEPH-RIPPENAAR

In this Anthology , the poems, amongst others, have captured the life of South Africans post apartheid. Written in English and Afrikaans many of the poems depict people doing ordinary things under extremely difficult circumstances. The author demonstrates fine insight into the challenges facing society, and the poems reflect that in a thoughtful way. Definitely worth reading.

EDWARD TAYLOR

I am so privileged to read this Anthology before print. I love the mix of languages, the rhythm which makes me want to read the poetry out loud, and the themes which are so pertinent for our South African people.

ANN ROWLEY-MORTON

George Hector's poetry is a successful blend of formal language usage and general language parlance, including dialect and colloquialism, that not only gives content to his poetry, but also conveys a relevant socio-political message.

SIMON BANDA

A thought-provoking debut collection of the experiences, observations, and perceptions of the poet that encapsulates the dreams and complexities of South African society. These poems will move you to connect in a meaningful way with your community.

GEORGINA VANACORE

The depth of the themes explores so many facets of the complexities of South African society. This Anthology draws on the experiences and insights of the writer, and causes one to reflect deeply.

AUGUSTINE "Okkie" MORKEL

* * *

MASTERPIECE

In the Earth I created for you,
I gave you my Masterpiece,
The light, the sky, the mighty seas,
It's there for you, my plants and trees.

In the Earth I created for you,
I made day and night rotation,
Light and darkness for every nation,
Work and rest for all creation.

In the Earth I created for you,
You have the seasons, your food supply,
It's there for you, you cannot deny,
It's all worked out perfectly, for you and I.

In the Earth I created for,
I planted mountains, from high to low,
Set my rivers on its meandering flow,
Lungs of oxygen for you to show.

But in your mad pursuit of meaningless riches,
Not caring or tending for my perfect soil,
My rivers are throttled with rubble, plastic, and oil,
Carbon waste of your empty toil.

But I will restore my Masterpiece,
The air will be cleaner,
The birds will be freer,

The fish will swim faster,
Even the Rhinos won't be a disaster.

And if Covid be my means to the end,
So be it.
For I will restore my Masterpiece,
And your great-grandchildren will,
Unlike you,
Cherish my Masterpiece anew.

✻ ✻ ✻

GHOEMAHARE

Spookasem, Candyfloss, en Ghoemahare,
One and the same.
Maar nou stry ons vir jare,
Who's to blame.

Vinkel, Koljander, Danya en Coriander,
One and the same,
Ons twis, maar die een is soos die ander,
Who's to blame.

Europees, African, Indian en Chinese,
One and the same,
Maar die target is eventueel, money please.
Who's to blame.

Kris, Slams, Hindu en Jood,
One and the same,
Hul copyright die goddelikheid tot die dood,
Who's to blame.

Coloured, Black, White, al die nasies,
One and the same,
En daar's net rooi tydens operasies,
Who's to blame.

En nou?
die doofheid,
die gierigheid,

die astrantheid,
die selfgeregtigheid,
die hate!
En nou ...
ons is almal op pad na stof
one and the same.
en ons almal is to blame.

* * *

GHOEMAHARE (FREE TRANSLATION)

Spookasem, Candyfloss, Ghoemahare,
one and the same
but yet there's conflict for years
who's to blame.

Fennel, Coriander, and Danya
one and the same,
we argue, but the one is like the other,
who's to blame.

European, African, Indian, Chinese,
one and the same,
but the target stays money please
who's to blame.

Christian, Muslim, Hindu and Jew,
one and the same,
they copyright religion up till death
who's to blame.

Coloured, Black, White, all nations,
one and the same,
and there's only red during surgery
who's to blame.

And now?

the deafness,
the coveting,
the arrogance,
the self-righteousness,
the hate!
And now...
We're all heading to dust
one and the same,
and we're all to blame.

❋ ❋ ❋

MY PA SE 4 X 4

My Pa is vandag lekker op sy stukke,
dis Maandag, en daar's baie scrap in die vullisblikke,
vandag se hy, vat ek jou saam,
nie hier nie, maar by die laanies in Sewendelaan,
en ek kyk na sy Checkers waentjie for sure,
After all, dis my Pa se 4 X 4.

Ek sit lekker op die waentjie se harde sitplek,
toe ek weer kyk, skree die merrem voertsek,
sy vloek my Pa, met rollers in haar hare,
sy accuse hom van inbreek, met lelike gebare!
en ek kyk na sy Checkers waentjie for sure,
After all, dis my Pa se 4 X 4.

Ek onthou my Pa se bakkie, 'n tydjie gelede,
hy't 'n kwaai job gehad in die vêrre verlede,
maar daai laanie by die werk was 'n horrible boss,
toe ek weer hoor, het hulle lelik uitgetos,
en ek kyk na sy Checkers waentjie for sure,
after all, dis my Pa se 4 X 4.

Maar wiet djy wat, daar's liefde in my hart,
al woon ons in 'n hokkie in my uncle se jaart,
en as ek skoolgaan, gaan ek mooi leer,
ek's vasberade om my te kwalifiseer,
jy sien,
ek worry nie van Pa se waentjie for sure,
want eendag is dit Fortuna, my eie 4 X 4.

My Notes On My Pa Se 4 X 4

This poem was inspired one day when I saw a very young child sitting in a shopping trolley, whilst his Dad was eking out a living collecting recyclable material from the dirtbins of the community which he could sell at the local recycling depot. The child seemed so contented and patient, happy to be with a parent, which clearly represents family to him.

The first stanza speaks of his Dad taking him with assuring him of rich pickings at the homes of the affluent, the second stanza addresses the stereotyping of that derogatory term, bin-pickers, the third stanza tells of the boy's memories of his Dad having had a good job, even owning his own car, but all that is now lost, and in the fourth stanza the boy explains that even though they live in a shack in the backyard of a relative, he is determined to do well at school to map a good future for himself.

The refrain of each of the first three stanzas goes as follows, And I look upon his Checkers trolley for sure, after all, it's my Dad's 4 X 4. (Checkers is a Supermarket chain in South Africa), but the variation of the refrain in stanza 4, goes as follows, One day it is Fortuna, my own 4 X 4.

* * *

ONS WORRY

Ons worry oor klip, brons,
en koper mannetjies,
wat pronk op sy perd,
en brekkerig,
soos 'n visionary pose
en doodstil staan
of sit,
en fokkol doen.

Hul staan yskoud
in die vriesende winter,
en voel nie 'n jit van pyn nie
word nooit honger
worry nie van healthcare
en quality education nie,
is nie ontstel,
as die voëls op hul kop
kak nie,
as jong manne
by die airport,
in sy bek
wil pis nie.

Maar daar's twee plase
by Brown en Orange,
daar's eksotiese name
soos Harare en Diepsloot,
waar kinders bewe van koudkry,

hul magies pyn van honger,
lus hulle so
vir 'n warm shower,
verlang hulle so na gumboots
met dik sokkies.

En ons worry van klip, brons,
en kopermannetjies.
Fokit!

❊ ❊ ❊

My Notes On Ons Worry

The Rhodes Must Fall events of 2018 in South Africa was a movement seeking to reconstruct the colonial vestiges at South African Universities. The vortex of anger expressed by the students and staff soon manifested itself in other actions, like the burning of Art works, and disruptions of lectures. This poem is a comment on the Movement. Below is free translation.

❊ ❊ ❊

WE WORRY (FREE TRANSLATION)

We worry about Stone, Bronze
and Copper mannikins,
sitting on his horse
posing like a visionary
and standing dead still
and does fuckall.

They stand ice cold
in the freezing Winter
does not feel anything
never becomes hungry
has no need of healthcare
or quality education,
isn't concerned
if the birds shit
on their heads
if young people
at airport entrances
wants to piss
in his mouth.

But there are two farms
at Brown and Orange
there's exotic names
like Harare and Diepsloot
where children shiver in the cold

their stomachs aching with hunger
long they so
for a hot shower
would love gumboots,
with thick socks.

And we worry about stone
and bronze and copper
mannikins
Fuckit!

＊　＊　＊

NEW NATION

I'd like to build a new nation,
a happy place, for you and me,
but please
can we make it on my terms,
I've had half a millennium
To be in charge,
And it worked perfectly,
For me.
So trust me,
I know all the answers,
I'm from Shakespeare, van Gogh,
Beethoven, and Bach,
Why change a winning recipe,
After all, it worked for me.

I know you like bra Hugh,
Jonathan Butler, Brenda Fassie
And others of your family tree.
But please,
I know all the answers,
It will be perfect, for you and me,
But especially me.

* * *

DIS AL WAT EK HET

'n Boksie metjies
'n paar druppels petrol
'n weggooityre van Dunlop
'n stinkbrand
In die middel van die pad,
Dis al wat ek het.

En as ek regtig
die moerin raak,
dan brand die kliniek,
die community centre
waar ons Saterdae dans,
die Prinsipaal se office blok
van my kind se skool.

Want ek skree al die tyd,
dat die lewe van armoede
en swaarkry
kan ek nie meer vat nie,
maar al wat ek kry
is TV footage,
en volgende jaar,
is dit weer dieselfde.

Maar vir nou,
Is dit al wat ek het,
Maar eendag,
Binnekort,

Gaan dit veel erger wees …

* * *

IT'S ALL I GOT (FREE TRANSLATION)

A box of matches
a few drops of petrol
a throwaway tyre from Dunlop
a burn of nausea
in the middle of the road
it's all I got.

And if I really get angry
then the clinic burns
the community centre
where we dance
on a Saturday is in flames
the Principal's office block
of my child's school
is reduced to ashes.

For I shout all the time,
that the life of poverty
and suffering,
I can't take it anymore
for all I get is TV footage,
And next year
It's more of the same.

But for now
It's all I got

but one day
soon,
it's going to be,
much worse...

* * *

EQUALITY THREE

We're only thrice equal,
one in the grave
where six feet of ground
makes us equal to
kings
queens
presidents
and peasants.

We're only thrice equal
two in the ballot box
where the cross we make
is of equal value to
kings
queens
presidents
or peasants.

We're only thrice equal
three before the judgement seat
where our works will be rewarded
be we
kings
queens
presidents
or peasants.

But why wait for the

grave
ballot box
judgement seat,
start anew
practice equality
in real life,
and maybe
we'll have,
Equality Four

* * *

FIRST FLIGHT

A fledgeling Sparrow landed on my lawn today,
and hop-hop-hop surveyed the challenge,
as if to play.

He shook his down, ready to fly,
for ahead was a mighty six-foot wall,
an awesome height,
but he was ready to try.

With courage and determination,
he fluttered his frail wings of flight,
and with magnificent power and sophistry,
ascended the incredible height.

From there he surveyed
his triumphant achievement,
looking down from the lofty heights
on which he set his sights.

O little Sparrows all over the World,
when you start your journey to be unfurled,
do it well,
with courage,
clothed in greatness,
for it all starts
in little flutters,
like A,B,C
and 1,2,3.

* * *

Dedicated to my four 2021 preschool grandkids, Joel, Hugo, Josh, and Hudson and penned in honour of all ECD and Foundation Phase teachers, both past and present.

* * *

MY NAAM IS LOGAN

My naam is Logan
ek's 'n TV Star,
my Ma se so
sy glo in my
ek's van die B en B,
ek's dapper en pragtig.

Al staan ek kaalvoet
met my een outfit
in Pastor se soplyn,
al eet ek so eenkeer,
'n stukkie hoender
'n special by Shoprite

Ja, my naam is Logan,
ek's 'n TV star,
my Ma se so,
sy glo in my.

* * *

MY NAME IS LOGAN (FREE TRANSLATION)

My name is Logan
I'm a TV star
My Mom says so,
She believes in me
I'm from the B and B
I'm bold and beautiful.

Though I stand barefeet
With my one outfit
In Pastor's soup line
And once in a while
Eat a piece of chicken
A special offer at Shoprite.

Yes, my name is Logan
I'm a TV star
My Mom says so
She believes in me.

* * *

Socio-Political Context

Logan was one of the hundreds of children who stood in the queue each Wednesday afternoon whilst we as a small group of the

Calvary Sanctuary Church in Wynberg, Cape Town, handed out soup and bread. We loved the words of St Augustine of Hippo, who exclaimed, Go forth, and proclaim the Gospel, and if necessary, use words. Logan to me represented the undying hope of parents for their children, no matter the dire poverty in which they live. Logan was one of the characters of the internationally popular TV soapie called, The Bold and the Beautiful.

OPSLAANTAMATIE

Die voeltjie vlieg hoog
in die hemelruim
en deponeer sy saadjie
op die komposhoop
van my tuin.

En toe ek weer kyk
Is daar grasgroen blare
'n geel blommetjie of drie
en opslaantamatie rank
sommerso
hoog in die takke.

Dis tamatiebredie,
tamatie en kaas
op wholewheat brood,
dis die helderrooi
in die tuna salad,
die lekker ryp smaak
van die burger, lettuce,
en kaassnytjie.

Alles van opslaantamatie,
sommerso,
uit die hemel geval.

❋ ❋ ❋

SELF-SOWING TOMATO (FREE TRANSLATION)

High in the skies
a bird flies
and deposits a seed
on the compost heap
of my garden,

And when I looked
there's green, green leaves
a yellow flower or three
and self-sowing tomato grows
just like that.

It's tomato stew
tomato and cheese
on wholewheat bread
the bright red
of the tuna salad
the lovely taste
of the burger with lettuce
and cheese.

All this from self-sowing tomato
falling from heaven
just like that!

* * *

A Note

I sought to find a translation for the Afrikaans term Opslaantamatie, searched dictionaries, up to Google Translate, but no luck. Using the network of Facebook friends and other acquaintances, the best we could come up with, is a sort of literal translation, Self-sowing tomato, which doesn't remotely capture the Afrikaans idiom. Indeed the wonder of language!

* * *

WHAT ARE YOU HOPING FOR?

What are you hoping for,
that the lockdown will end
that the curve will flatten
that we can remove our masks
and wash our hands less.

What are you hoping for,
that businesses shall thrive,
slave wages shall continue,
and the highways shall stay clogged,
with stinking carbon fumes,
really, what are you hoping for.

What are you hoping for,
that the system
you've come to love so much.
that gave you such largesse
and comforts of affluence,
centrally heated homes,
next to freezing shacks
and crates next to bedsides,
to step on,
just in case,
it rained in.

You can hope,

but everything,
as you know it,
is over.

A new world
is being born,
seek to enter it,
embrace it,
love it,
it's the only way,
and guess what,
we'll all live better.

❊ ❊ ❊

SUIKERBEKKIE EN STRELITZIA

Strelitzia, blou, geel, en pers,
vlieg in swerms van skakerings
in die laat Herfs seisoen
pronk in prag en perfeksie
en verwelkom Suikerbekkie
hy van velvetvere, en perfekte snawel
om sy nektaar te kom drink
pure plesier van perfeksie soetigheid.

Hulle werk so mooi saam,
die een verskaf soetigheid en lewensbron
die ander ontvang bestuiwing,
die belofte van 'n nuwe lewe,
saadjies wat sal ontkiem,
en prag en perfeksie,
sal voortbring.

Dankie vir die les,
Suikerbekkie en Strelitzia,
In vrede en harmonie
leef julle saam,
en beide trek voordeel,
soetigheid en lewensbron,
bestuiwing en nuwe lewe,
in vredevolle harmonie.

Here help my
die volgende keer
as selfsug en nydigheid
by my opkom
dat ek sal dink
aan Suikerbekkie en Strelitzia
wat in harmonie
en perfeksie
saamleef.

* * *

SUGARBIRD AND STRELITZIA (FREE TRANSLATION)

Strelitzia, blue, yellow, purple,
Flying in swarms of colours
In late fall.
Pose, pretty, and perfect,
Welcomes Sugarbird
He of Velvet feathers and perfect beak
To drink of the Nectar
Pure, Pleasant, Perfect, Sweetness.

They work together so well
The one giving sweetness and life
The other getting pollinated
The promise of new life
Seeds that will germinate
And more beauty and perfection provide.

Thank you for the lesson
Sugarbird and Strelitzia
In peace and harmony
You co-exist
In perfect symbiosis
Give sweetness and nutrition
Pollination and new life
Perfect, peaceful, harmonious.

Lord help me
If selfishness and covetousness
Arise in me.
That I shall consider
Sugarbird and Strelitzia
That in harmony
And perfection
Co-exist.

* * *

HIDDEN TREASURE

Miskien, onder in die vullisblik,
is daar 'n hidden treasure,
'n diamond ring, goue earrings,
of wie weet, 'n honderd rand noot,
wat iemand, by mistake
in die vullisblik laat val het.

In die tussentyd, skarrel ek,
vir plastic melkbottels, Coke empties
5 litre onnodig duur water kannetjies.
Ek doen my plig, unlike the rich
om die environment te save
en die landfill te beskerm.

Vandag, hopelik 'n goeie dag,
gaan ek R50 of so maak
by die recycling depot,
daam iets, om my laaities
'n halwe brood, Sunshine D,
en jem te koop.
En miskien, maybe, is daar change,
vir 'n lekker dop cheap wyn.

Maar eendag, gaan ek die jackpot slaan,
'n diamond ring, goue earrings,
'n twee honderd rand noot,
'n Hidden Treasure,
Onder in die vullisblik.

Meanwhile, skarrel ek maar aan.

* * *

HIDDEN TREASURE (FREE TRANSLATION)

Maybe, at the bottom of the bin
There's a hidden treasure
A diamond ring, gold earrings
Or who knows,
A hundred dollar bill
That somebody, by mistake
Dropped in the bin.

In the meanwhile, I scratch around
For plastic milkbottles, Coke empties
Unnecessarily expensive water bottles.
But I do my bit, unlike the rich
To save the environment
To protect the landfill.

Today, hopefully
I'll have a good day,
Making R50 or so
At the re-cycling depot
Something for my kids
Half a loaf, maybe marge
Even apricot jam
And who knows
A nippy of wine.

But one day, I'll hit the jackpot

A diamond ring, gold earrings,
A two hundred dollar bill
A hidden treasure
At the bottom of the bin
Meanwhile, I'll scratch around.

* * *

RAINDROP

After day zero
the dams are full
to overflowing
one raindrop at a time.

So do your little bit
to achieve the glory
of life giving water
for all,
by small deeds
in your corner
of the dam.

Our life dams
need not be empty
if all
in their corner of the dam
let their raindrops fall.

✳ ✳ ✳

SIPHO AND GOGO

Mischievous, wide-eyed,
making sense of this new world,
of English, Maths, and worse still,
the foreign language of Afrikaans,
in this world entered Sipho,
just nine years old.

Dismissive diagnosis and analysis
followed him, like inattentive,
fidgety, distracted,
even lazy, and slow!
that's how the teachers described Sipho,
just nine years old.

But on the football field,
nimble-footed, a mesmerizing
body swerve, an accurate shot
from the left foot, where his one boot was,
this was Sipho, living his dream,
and then the taxi rode away.

Sipho and I, alone at school,
so off to Gugs rode,
left was often right, or wrong,
stop streets meant nothing
and so also the traffic lights,
hopelessly lost we were,
then Sipho found the landmark,

the taxi rank,
next to Gogo's house.

Warm grateful eyes greeted me,
continual thanks, tenderly spoken,
from Gogo, in her wood and iron house,
just big enough for a single bed,
a makeshift table,
with a Primus Stove,
two roughly made shelves,
a pot, and pan, a few plates,
and recycled jars, for some
sugar, tea, and powdered milk.

Shyly Sipho kissed his Gogo,
receiving a warm embrace,
changed into casual clothes,
and with great pride, neatly folded
the pants, blazer, and shirt,
and placed it
where all his earthly belongings were,
a carboard box,
under Gogo's bed.

Fighting back tears,
my heart bursting,
I greeted Gogo and Sipho,
and drove away,
hanging my head in shame,
all those workshops,
brainstorming sessions,
political discourse, liberation theology,
swotting education theory,
into the deep of the night,
for I came to realise,
it meant nothing,

for I failed the test
of seek first to understand
than to be understood,*
a study engaged in
over a long weekend.

*With acknowledgement to Steven Covey, The Seven Habits of Highly Successful People

* * *

PEETMA

Ek bewe en bibber in die Winterkoue,
die hoendervleis slaan uit tot binne in my moue,
en ek dink van 'n jersey 22 jaar gelede.
daar doer in die oue verlede.

Dis blou, snoesig, met cables so deftig
gebrei deur my Peetma, laas jaar was sy neëntig
sy sing reeds in die kerkkoor, 'n soprano so pragtig,
haar liefde vir Jesus dra haar deur, Hy's so magtig.

En ek trek aan my jersey
onder my blanket top.
en die warmte van haar liefde,
maak die koue stop.

❊ ❊ ❊

My Note

My late Godmother, my Aunt, Iris Olivier, was a remarkable woman. She had an unquenchable fountain of love, and I was amongst those, many, who drank from the fountain of her love. She made a commitment for my spiritual well-being when I was a baby-in-arms at my Baptism in 1948, when she stood as my Godmother, and she kept to her promise for 73 years up to her passing in 2021. The jersey I refer to in the poem she gave me on my 50th birthday, and I also have a 60th and 70th edition, knitted in her 90th year!

* * *

FLY!

All I do each day,
is fly and flutter,
and play,
then I fly!

And when I feed,
never more than my need,
not given to greed,
enjoying every seed,
and then I fly!

And just one branch,
one tree.
to rest or sleep
extra space to keep
for them and me,
and then I fly!

And then I build a nest
reserved for the very best
who will know
to play and feed
and grow,
and then they fly!

* * *

ONE WITH THE EARTH

Whether in a coffin,
a shroud
or even a casket
of scatter ashes,
Mother Earth will receive you,
embrace you
become one with you
share her warmth with you
place you in permanent comfort,
undisturbed,
for a very long time,
up to close
to eternity.

She's your best friend
your only true friend,
never rejecting you.

And now I wonder,
this perfectly
loving friend,
who will never
reject you,
will care for you,
look after you,
for ages,

receive you
in her bosom,
is so neglected
so polluted
so exploited,
as though dispensable
and replaceable.

But it's all
you've ever got,
and ever will have.

❋ ❋ ❋

THE SPARROW AND THE TURTLEDOVES

The Sparrows and the Turtledoves,
side by side, in my yard,
happily receive the gift of seeds,
enough for everyone needs.

Alongside each other, mixing easily
they share the blessing, fluttering happily,
taking enough, without a fight,
fuelling up, for majestical flight.

And when they fly off into the sky,
they say, there's been enough for you and I,
and that which is left behind,
it's for others, of my kind.

What's wrong with us
we gorge ourselves to overweight,
and gather for ourselves in a great fight,
we are burdened down, lost our flight,
and our dreams, kindness and beauty,
Are totally out of sight.

✽ ✽ ✽

MOERSE PLAAS

Jare en jare gelede, klim Grootpa op sy perd,
en ry hektaars plat vir al wat dit's werd,
daar's nie 'n siel in sig oor al die pleine,
en hy se in sy hart, dis alles myne.

En die First Nation kyk verstom,
en wonder, wat is sy storie,
hy's een man, is hy fokken dom
hy gaan hom vrek werk, in sy glorie,
min te weet, hy't dit uitgewerk,
die dopstelsel, al sit hy voor in die kerk.

En nou sit ek
met 'n meulsteen
om my nek,
my Pa se Moerse Plaas.

Selfvoldaan, staan Pa met trots en kyk,
hy stoot sy bors uit, ek het dit alles bereik,
ek het hard gewerk, my koningryk opgebou,
aan my godsdiens, was ek altyd getrou.

En in die afstand, in die grotte so diep,
sit die Khoisan, verstom oor die spektakel,
en se vir homself, jy's een man
al die land wat jy vat, loop uit op 'n debakel.
En oor die jare het hy dit uitgewerk,
die dopstelsel, al sit hy voor in die kerk.

En nou sit ek
met 'n meulsteen
om my nek
my Pa se Moerse Plaas.

En Pa sê, kyk my wingerdlande
dis die werk van my eie hande,
my honderde skape, varke, en beeste
veral laasgenoemde, die wins is die meeste.

En die volkies werk dat hulle sweet,
maar hul plek ken, dit moet hulle weet,
en op my Stinkhouttafel staan ingevoerde wyne
'n fees voorberei, vir ek en myne,
maar die system het dit noukeurig uitgewerk,
die dopstelsel, al sit Pa voor in die kerk.

Maar nou sit ek
met 'n meulsteen
om my nek
my Pa se Moerse Plaas.

2022 bid ek, Here kan U 'n uitkoms bring,
die armoede en swaarkry het ons omring,
maar Grootpa se plaas het ons so baie gegee
privaatskole, strandhuise, blue chip shares, en alles
    daarmee.

En regoor die land, dis die mense wat ly
die gaping tussen ryk en arm beteken swaarkry,
en die pyn en die woede raak erger by die dag
dis 'n sweer wat seermaak, van geslag tot geslag
maar demmit, dis nie hoe dit behoort,
die dopstelsel legacy, die system, leef voort.

En nou sit ek
met 'n meulsteen
om my nek
my Pa se Moerse Plaas.

* * *

LEGACY

Legacy is not the size of your estate,
the riches you struggled to accumulate,
No, legacy are values left behind
abundant love in you they find,
thinking of you, forgetting never,
in their hearts, always forever.

Legacy is a smile in your heart,
a cherished memory, never to depart,
a book read shared, sitting on a boat,
telling stories as on the waters you float,
the excitement of your coffee-grinder singing
the sweetest sound in your ears ringing.

Legacy are grandkids you get to know,
the unleashing of potential as you watch them grow,
that warm contented feeling as your own you loved,
will continue as by yours they are loved,
for you know good people they will become
as they build on your love from day one.

Legacy are memories of values into eternity,
diligence, compassion, loyalty, love for humanity,
no matter life's grind, just be kind,
wherever yourself you find, keep a pure mind,
for the most beautiful thing ever you will find,

is the cherished legacy, left behind.

JUST A PENTUNIA

Mom didn't much bother or fuss,
in fact, she never made demands on us,
but she loved the simple things of life,
a chat, a story, a life without strife.

She loved the simple things you see,
Cream Crackers, cheese, a peck of tomato,
and Five Roses, the best cup of tea,
you had to have it, before you go.

Eleven children, my Mom she had,
and guess what, no one turned out bad,
and this what each one knew,
all are loved, to all she was true.

We never missed out her Christmas garden,
of a few punnets of Petunias.
She was absolutely delighted,
and when the first bloom greeted,
she became so so excited.

But for her,
that's more than enough,
Just a Petunia
of love,
of care
of making time
of thoughtfulness,

Just a Petunia.

* * *

WIET DJY

Wiet djy hoe isit om te skarrel
om te hoop op anders se weggooigoed
regtigwaar, wat fokol vir hulle meen
maar vir my laaities is dit miskien rama
of wie weet, djem op hulle brood
of so 'n sopie koue Jive.

Wiet djy, hoe swaar is my oorgelaaide trollie
En as die brug oor die spoorweglyn wink
Dan pyn my rug alreeds
Val die sweetkorrels op die grond
Maar wat kan ek doen, ek druk deur,
'n ou moet survive, en die laaities wag.

OK, ek kom van daai background
Waar die feeding scheme van die skool
My enigste maaltyd was
En ek sit en droom op die skoolbanke
Ek wonder hoe suksesvol my Pa was
Met vandag se skarrel

❊ ❊ ❊

SOON

Soon, in the wink of an eye,
one day, or sixty years from now,
you'll be taken out of life,
you might not even say goodbye,
all will end.

There will be no more gatherings,
no more building,
no more good works,
for all that's left
are memories
of others,
of you.

So cherish every moment,
to build,
to work,
to serve,
but above all,
to love.

❋ ❋ ❋

COCO

No matter what
when I've been out,
whether at work
or fishing,
or at the movies
or visiting life-long friends,
she seeks me out,
wherever I am,
does a waggietail,
puts her moist snout
on my leg,
or trouser pants
and says hi,
glad to see you,
and then wanders off.

She's Coco, my Sharpei,
my friend and entertainer,
for 12 years now.

And we never had an argument
or even a mild disagreement,
just unconditional love.

* * *

LOCKDOWNED FOR GOOD

We're lockdowned for good,
we don't like it, but what can we do,
it's hectic, both for me and you,
and you can argue till you're blue,
there's no alternative, and that's true,
Yes, we're lockdowned for good.

We're lockdowned for good,
homecooked food, eating better,
respecting the Law to the letter,
focused on things that matter,
appreciating local is lekker,
Yes, we're lockdowned for good.

But we should be lockdowned for good,
to have learnt that it's good,
to be lockdowned for good,
for if we don't change,
and see the world differently,
we might as well,
be lockdowned for good.

EPILOGUE

QUO VADIS

One of my closest confidantes and one who constantly inspires me to stay true to our calling is Rev Les Mathys, Minister of the Congregational Church in Gleemoor, Athlone, Cape Town. His last rallying cry to me was contained in an email sent on 16 November 2023 wherein he encourages me to never grow weary of doing good. He addresses the issue of steadfastly pursuing Restorative Justice, staying true to the Constitution of our country in its Preamble whereby we are implored to work towards righting the wrongs of the past.

I am encouraged, by Les, amongst many others, to strive to never let my pen become silent, but continue to address the issues of the day.

Bless you Les.

Aluta Continua. The struggle for a more just society continues. We cannot go on this way whereby 3 million of our children go to bed hungry each day, where 60% of our young people between the ages of 18 and 24 do not have work,

MORE VOICES PLEASE!!

George Hector

18 November 2023

* * *

ABOUT THE AUTHOR

George Hector

I was born on the 6th of May 1948 on a chicken farm in the Western Cape, South Africa, the fourth of eleven children. My Mom was a housewife and my Dad, a schoolteacher. Educated at the local Primary and High Schools, I studied for my teaching Diploma at Hewat College of Education, and furthered my qualifications at The University of the Western Cape. After twelve years of class teaching at Sunnyside Primary School in Athlone, Cape Town I was promoted to Headmaster. After 38 years in the profession, I sought new horizons, working as the Executive Secretary to the President of the International Cricket Council in 2006 and 2007, lecturing and mentoring in-service teachers pursuing the Advanced Certificate in School Management and Leadership from 2007 to 2015 at both UCT and UWC, was appointed the Administrative Head of a start-up Independent School called Grassroots Preparatory, 2017 to 2019, based on the Finnish Model, and subsequent to that have been following one of my greatest passions, running a small horticultural business called H3 Nurseries, and am still busy.

I am the Dad of three boys and three girls, and like all 75 year olds, dote on my grandchildren, 8 of them.

Printed in Great Britain
by Amazon

33330708R00046